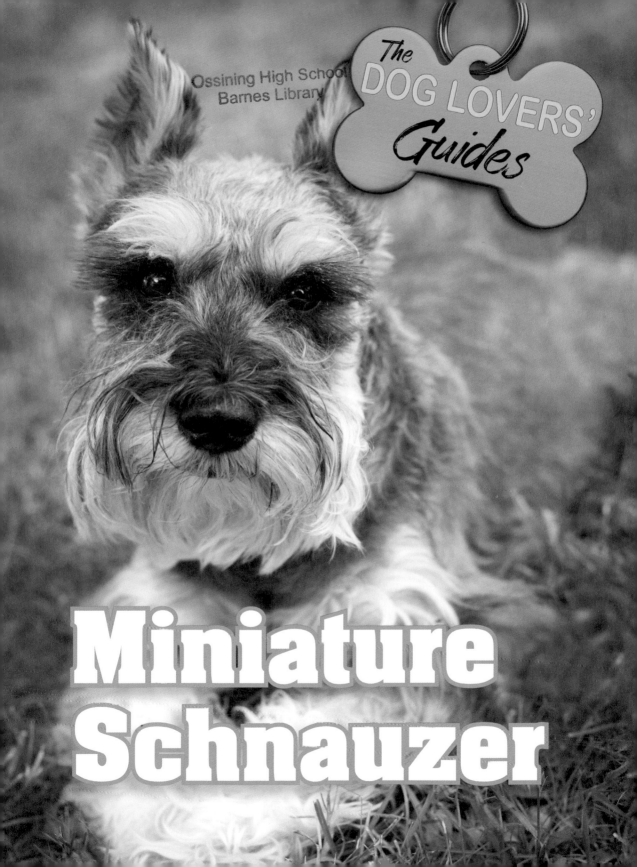

The
DOG LOVERS'
Guides

Miniature
Schnauzer

The Dog Lovers' Guides

Beagle
Boxer
Bulldog
Cavalier King Charles Spaniel
Chihuahua
Cocker Spaniel
Dachshund
French Bulldog
German Shepherd
Golden Retriever
Labrador Retriever
Miniature Schnauzer
Poodle
Pug
Rottweiler
Siberian Husky
Shih Tzu
Yorkshire Terrier

Miniature Schnauzer

By Jeanette Wilson

Mason Crest
450 Parkway Drive, Suite D
Broomall, PA 19008
www.masoncrest.com

© 2018 by Mason Crest, an imprint of National Highlights, Inc.

Printed and bound in the United States of America.

Series ISBN: 978-1-4222-3848-6
Hardback ISBN: 978-1-4222-3946-9
EBook ISBN: 978-1-4222-7842-0

First printing
1 3 5 7 9 8 6 4 2

Cover photograph by Littleny/Dreamstime.com.

Library of Congress Cataloging-in-Publication Data is on file with the publisher.

QR Codes disclaimer:

You may gain access to certain third-party content ("Third-Party Sites") by scanning and using the QR Codes that appear in this publication (the "QR Codes"). We do not operate or control in any respect any information, products, or services on such Third-Party Sites linked to by us via the QR Codes included in this publication, and we assume no responsibility for any materials you may access using the QR Codes. Your use of the QR Codes may be subject to terms, limitations, or restrictions set forth in the applicable terms of use or otherwise established by the owners of the Third-Party Sites. Our linking to such Third-Party Sites via the QR Codes does not imply an endorsement or sponsorship of such Third-Party Sites, or the information, products, or services offered on or through the Third-Party Sites, nor does it imply an endorsement or sponsorship of this publication by the owners of such Third-Party Sites.

Contents

Key Icons to Look For

Sidebars: This boxed material within the main text allows readers to build knowledge, gain insights, explore possibilities, and broaden their perspectives by weaving together additional information to provide realistic and holistic perspectives.

Educational Videos: Readers can view videos by scanning our QR codes, providing them with additional educational content to supplement the text. Examples include news coverage, moments in history, speeches, iconic moments, and much more!

Series Glossary of Key Terms: This back-of-the-book glossary contains terminology used throughout this series. Words found here increase the reader's ability to read and comprehend higher-level books and articles in this field.

Chapter 1

Introducing the Miniature Schnauzer

Smart, lively, and playful, the Miniature Schnauzer is a superb companion. Looking out from under his bushy eyebrows, he is always on the alert, keen to take part in everything. He also has a gentle side, and will give you boundless love and affection.

The Miniature Schnauzer was bred down from the larger Standard Schnauzer, a dog valued as an intelligent herder, a formidable ratter, and a fearless guard dog. The Mini Schnauzer's primary role was always as a companion, but he retains many of the characteristics of his ancestors.

Physical characteristics

The Miniature Schnauzer comes in a very convenient size. He measures 12 to 14 inches (30 to 35 cm) at the top of the shoulder, which makes him a substantial little dog—bigger and more robust than the Toy breeds, but small enough to adapt to any size home.

He has a neat, square body, which is complemented by a head roughly shaped like a brick. He moves with a forward-reaching, purposeful gait, which sums up his outgoing personality.

The coat is harsh and wiry, but it is the furnishings—the areas of longer hair—that make the Mini Schnauzer so distinctive. In contrast to the tight-fitting coat on his body, he has longer hair on the

Miniature Schnauzer Colors

The Miniature Schnauzer comes in several color combinations.

Salt and pepper: This is the most common coat color, and is unique to Schnauzers. The guard hairs on the topcoat are banded to create a mosaic of black-gray coloring. The furnishings are lighter in color. Puppies are born with a dark coat, and it lightens as they mature. There is considerable variation in shades of salt and pepper in adult Miniature Schnauzers.

Black: A striking pure black.

Black and silver: The black body coat contrasts with silver markings.

White: Not seen in the USA, this color is now recognized in most other countries.

legs, underside, and hindquarters. The longer hair on his head forms remarkably bushy eyebrows and a distinguished-looking mustache and beard. It all makes him look a little bit like a Civil War general.

Schnauzers and allergies

The Miniature Schnauzer's coat does not shed in the same way as most other breeds, so he is potentially a good choice for people who are allergic to dogs.

However, there is a minimal amount of shedding, and sometimes allergies are caused by canine dander or saliva, so there are no guarantees for allergy sufferers.

The best plan is to spend some time with Miniature Schnauzers and see how you react before you make a commitment to buy a puppy.

Temperament

What can you expect if you bring a Miniature Schnauzer into your home? Every dog is an individual, but there is one thing you can be sure of: Your life will never be quite the same.

The Mini Schnauzer is a relatively small dog, but he has a huge personality. He finds the world a fascinating place and wants to investigate everything, and everyone, that comes his way. He is one of the most companionable of breeds; he simply wants to be where his people are. He must learn to cope with spending time on his own, but he will be utterly miserable if he is excluded for long periods.

He is also an excellent watchdog. The

Mini Schnauzer takes his guarding duties very seriously and will be ever ready to warn you of approaching strangers. This is great, as long as you do not allow it to get out of hand. A warning bark is desirable; a dog who will not be quiet, or one who runs up and down the fence barking continuously, is not. This all comes down to training, which is extremely important when taking on a Miniature Schnauzer.

Family dog

Children and Miniature Schnauzers go well together, but you must ensure that a sense of mutual respect is established from the start. Children must learn not to tease or to play games that provoke over-excitement. They must also understand that there are times when a dog should not be disturbed, particularly when he is eating and sleeping.

A Miniature Schnauzer must learn to cooperate with all members of his human family, no matter how small they are. Interactions should be closely supervised, so he learns that jumping up, mouthing, and nipping are not acceptable behaviors.

If you get relations off to a good start, you will be rewarded with a wonderful companion who is loving and affectionate with all members of his family.

Life expectancy

We are fortunate that the Miniature Schnauzer is a healthy breed with a good life expectancy. Most will reach their early teens, and some may live even longer.

Schnauzer history

The Miniature Schnauzer is a bred-down version of the Standard Schnauzer, a medium dog measuring 17.5 to 19.5 inches (44 to 50 cm) at the highest point of the shoulders. The Standard is the original member of the Schnauzer family. A type of dog very similar to the Standard Schnauzer was popular in the 14th or 15th century in southern Germany, where he was used as an all-purpose farm dog. He worked as a drover, moving livestock from place to place, was a formidable ratter in the stables, and was a useful watchdog. This versatile dog would also pull a cart to market if required.

There is no question that the Schnauzer has a long history. Albrecht Durer depicted a Schnauzer in a 1492 watercolor titled *Madonna with the Many Animals*.

In the 19th century, German breeders added new breeds to the mix, such as the Standard Poodle and the Wirehaired Pinscher, to create the breed we now know as the Standard Schnauzer. *Schnauze* is the German word for muzzle, and this was the dog with a beard and mustache on his muzzle.

Mini Schnauzer history

Giant Schnauzer

The giant variety was developed in the early 20th century when the Germans were experimenting with the most suitable breeds to use as police dogs. Breeders crossed black Great Danes with the Standard Schnauzer, with the aim of producing a large, impressive dog with strong protective instincts. His role was as a deterrent, barking a warning rather than being overtly aggressive.

Miniature Schnauzer

The smallest member of the Schnauzer family was developed to be a more compact version of the Standard Schnauzer. They were particularly sought after as a ratter in the home and farm, as well as being an alert watchdog.

In many instances, downsizing a breed entails selecting the smallest representatives for breeding. But this was not the case with the Miniature Schnauzer. In the late 19th century, good examples of Standards were crossed with smaller breeds, such as the Affenpinscher and the Pomeranian, as well as the rough-coated German Terrier and the Poodle, to achieve the perfect Schnauzer in miniature.

Establishing the breed

The earliest record of a Miniature Schnauzer was a black female named Findel, born in October 1888. In 1895, the first breed club was formed in Cologne, Germany, although it accepted several types of dogs.

World Wars I and II were hard on dog breeding, particularly in Europe, and some breeds were nearly lost. But Miniature Schnauzers became popular in the United States between the wars, and were well established. Mini Schnauzers have been bred in the United States since 1925 and were officially recognized by the American Kennel Club in 1926; the American Miniature Schnauzer Club was formed in 1933.

Miniature Schnauzers consistently rank among the top 20 most popular AKC breeds, and are the most popular terriers. Celebrity owners past and present include Janet Jackson, Paul Newman, Rob Lowe, Steve McQueen, Mary Tyler Moore, Bruce Lee, Sugar Ray Leonard, Katherine Heigl, Avril Lavigne, and Amy Grant.

Chapter 2

What Should a Mini Schnauzer Look Like?

The Miniature Schnauzer, so smart and full of character, draws admiring glances wherever she goes. In the show ring, when she is groomed to perfection, she stands out among all the show dogs. What makes a Mini Schnauzer so special?

The aim of breeders is to produce dogs who are sound, healthy, typical examples of their breed, in terms of both looks and temperament. To achieve this, they are guided by a breed standard, which is a written blueprint describing what a perfect example of the breed should look like.

Of course, there is no such thing as a "perfect" dog, but breeders aspire to produce dogs who conform as closely as possible to the breed standard, which describes a dog who is sound and healthy in every way. In the show ring, judges use the breed standard to assess

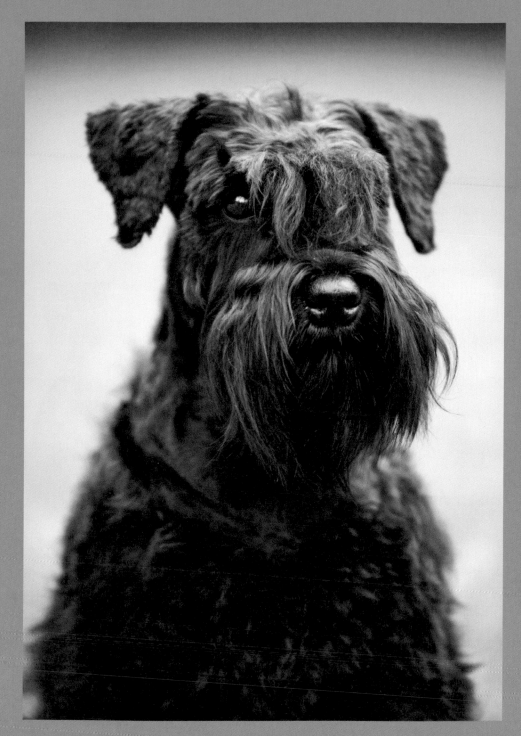

the dogs before them, and it is the dog who, in their opinion, comes closest to the ideal, that wins top honors.

This has significance beyond the sport of showing, because the dogs who win in the ring are the ones who are bred. The winners of today are therefore responsible for passing on their genes to future generations and preserving the breed in its best form.

General appearance

Small, sturdy, and robust, the Miniature Schnauzer is well balanced and appears smart and stylish. She should be sturdy and look like a terrier, not like a Toy dog. In terms of shape, the Mini Schnauzer is almost square—her body length is equal to her height at the shoulders—and she has a keen, alert expression.

Size

Both dogs and bitches should be 12 to 14 inches (30 to 35 cm) at the withers, which is the highest point of the shoulder.

Head and skull

The Miniature Schnauzer is known as a head breed, meaning that this one of his outstanding features. The head is strong and rectangular. Its width diminishes slightly from ears to eyes, and again to the tip of the nose.

The top of the skull is flat and fairly long. There should be no wrinkles on the forehead.

The stop, which is where the muzzle meets the skull, is moderate, to accentuate the prominent eyebrows. The muzzle is powerful, ending in a blunt line, with a bristly mustache and chin whiskers. The nose is black with wide nostrils.

Ears

The ears should be set high on the skull. They are in balance with the head and not exaggerated in length.

Early on, some Miniature Schnauzers had cropped ears, and this practice continued for much of the breed's history. Today, ear cropping is not done in most countries and is illegal in many. The American breed standard allows dogs to be show with their ears either cropped or natural. Cropped ears are cut into triangles with pointed tips, and the inner edges should be perpendicular. If not cropped, they should be small and V-shaped, folding close to the skull and dropping forward toward the temples.

Eyes

The eyes are small, oval, deep-set, and forward-facing—an impression enhanced by the bushy eyebrows. They are dark brown, with a keen expression.

Mouth

The jaws are strong and the teeth meet in a scissors bite. That means the teeth on the upper jaw closely overlap the teeth on the lower jaw when the mouth is closed.

Neck

The neck is strong and nobly arched. It blends smoothly into the shoulders; the skin on the throat is tight-fitting.

Body

The chest is moderately broad, with the bottom of the chest extending at least to the elbows. The ribs extend well back. The back is strong with a topline that slopes slightly from the withers (the highest point of the shoulders) to the base of the tail.

Forequarters

The front legs are straight and parallel when viewed from all sides. The elbows are close to the body. The sloping shoulders are well muscled, but the shoulder blade lies close against the rib cage. The pasterns, which act as the shock absorbers on the front legs, are short and springy.

Hindquarters

The hindquarters are strong and muscled; they are well bent at the stifle (the dog's knee). The hocks (equivalent to our ankles) are strong and very well angulated, turning neither in nor out. The hindquarters should never be higher than the shoulders.

Feet

These are short, round, and cat-like with thick black pads. The toes are arched and compact.

Tail

The tail is set high on the back, and is of moderate length, thick at the base and tapering toward the top. The Miniature Schnauzer

is among a number of breeds of dogs whose tails were traditionally docked from birth. The idea, originally, was to prevent injuries. Nowadays, the only reason for docking a Schnauzer's tail is for cosmetic purposes, and the practice is banned in many countries. However, docking is still allowed in the USA, and at dog shows, Mini Schnauzers are shown with tails docked only long enough to be clearly visible over the backline of the body. If you prefer not to dock your dog's tail, she is still a great pet.

Gait or movement

When the Miniature Schnauzer is trotting, her forelegs should reach out, with the driving power coming from behind. The movement should appear free, balanced, and vigorous.

Coat

The breed is double-coated with a dense undercoat and a harsh, wiry topcoat. The furnishings—the longer hair on the head and legs—should be fairly thick, but not silky. In the show ring, the head, neck, ears, chest, tail, and body coat must be plucked.

Color

The traditional colors for the Miniature Schnauzer are salt and pepper, black and silver, and black. Salt and pepper is a combination of black and white banded hairs and solid black and white unbanded hairs; the banded hairs should predominate. All shades are acceptable.

Black and silver is a striking color combination; dogs are solid black with silver markings on the eyebrows, muzzle, chest, legs, and under the tail.

Temperament

The breed standard says, "The typical Miniature Schnauzer is alert and spirited, yet obedient to command. He is friendly, intelligent and willing to please. He should never be overaggressive or timid. "

Summing up

Although the majority of Mini Schnauzers are pet dogs and will never be exhibited in the show ring, it is important that breeders strive for perfection and try to produce dogs who adhere as closely as possible to the Breed Standard. This ensures that the Miniature Schnauzer remains sound in mind and body, and retains the unique characteristics of this very special breed.

Chapter 3

What Do You Want From Your Mini Schnauzer?

There are hundreds of dog breeds to choose from, so how can you be sure the Miniature Schnauzer is the right one for you? Before you run out and get a Mini Schnauzer, weigh the pros and cons and make sure you are 100 percent certain this breed suits your lifestyle.

Companion

The Miniature Schnauzer has inherited working traits from his ancestors. He is an excellent guard dog and vermin catcher. But it is in the role of companion that he excels. The Mini Schnauzer is a natural fit in a family, and he thrives on being part of a busy household.

However, his working history does continue to play a part in his makeup. The Standard Schnauzer was valued for his adaptability

and his ability to think for himself, and you will see these traits in the miniature version.

The Mini Schnauzer will fit in with all types of families and lifestyles. He is good with children and will be an enthusiastic playmate. He will equally suit older owners with a more sedate lifestyle. He will be loving and affectionate with all members of the family, but you may find that he has a special favorite he tends to hang out with.

Although you want to encourage your Mini Schnauzer to bond closely with his human family, make sure you train him to accept some times spent on his own. This is a breed that can become too dependent on people, and without proper training he may become very anxious when he is left alone. This will take the form of constant barking or destructive behavior, and so it is vital to start his training early. From the day your puppy comes home, get him used

to spending short periods on his own—ideally when he is safe and secure in an indoor crate—and he will understand that although you go away, you always come back.

Watchdog

The Miniature Schnauzer is a great watchdog—and the sound he makes suggests a far bigger dog. This is a plus if you want to be warned about visitors approaching, but make sure you keep it under control. A Miniature Schnauzer will start barking—but he won't necessarily stop unless you train him to be quiet when you say so, and then reward him for cooperating.

Show dog

Do you have ambitions to exhibit your Miniature Schnauzer in the show ring? This is a specialist sport, and you must have the right dog to start with.

If you plan to show your Mini Schnauzer, you need to track down a show-quality puppy, then train him so he will perform in the show ring, and accept the detailed hands-on examination of the judge. You will also have to become an expert groomer, or hire a professional. The Miniature Schnauzer is very high-maintenance in terms of show presentation, so you will need to be truly dedicated to this highly specialized art.

It is also important to bear in mind that not every puppy with show potential develops into a top-quality show dog, so you must be prepared to love your Mini Schnauzer and give him a home for life, even if he doesn't make the grade in the show ring.

Sports dog

If you are interested in competing in one of the canine sports, the intelligent Miniature Schnauzer will be more than willing. He likes to use his brain and will make his mark in obedience, rally O, and agility. Other sports tap into his ratter heritage, such as earthdog and barn hunt.

What does your Mini Schnauzer want from you?

A dog cannot speak for himself, so we need to view the world from a canine perspective and figure out what a Miniature Schnauzer needs live a happy, contented, and fulfilling life.

Time and commitment

First of all, a Mini Schnauzer needs a commitment that you will care for him for his entire life—guiding him through his puppyhood, enjoying his adulthood, and being there for him in his later years. If all dog owners were prepared to make this pledge, there would hardly be any dogs in rescue.

The Miniature Schnauzer was bred primarily to be a companion dog, and this is what he must be. If you cannot give your Mini Schnauzer the time and commitment he needs and deserves, it's probably best to put off owning a dog until your circumstances change.

Practical matters

The Miniature Schnauzer is an adaptable dog and will cope with varying amounts of exercise. He has the energy and endurance to enjoy long hikes, but he is equally content with shorter outings, particularly if there is an element of variety. However, it is important to bear in mind that this is an active little dog and his exercise needs must not be neglected.

When it comes to coat care, you need to understand what you are taking on. This is a high-maintenance breed, and this applies to pet dogs as well as show dogs. A pet dog needs to be clipped regularly, and show dogs must undergo the lengthy process of being hand-stripped, as well as being trimmed to enhance the unique Schnauzer look. As a pet owner, you must budget for the services of a professional groomer to keep your Miniature Schnauzer clean and comfortable, as well as making sure he looks his best.

Mental stimulation

The Miniature Schnauzer is quick to learn, but this is something of a double-edged sword, because he will be equally quick to pick up both good and bad habits. A well-trained Schnauzer is a joy to own, but you cannot leave this clever dog to his own devices. Although he

doesn't have an ounce of malice in his make-up, a Mini Schnauzer with no rules or boundaries is not fun to live with. He will become very demanding, and if he doesn't get what he wants, he may bark at you until you give in.

As a responsible owner, you must set the house rules and apply them fairly and consistently. You must train him using positive methods, so he is happy to cooperate.

You must also give him the opportunity to use his brain. It does not matter what you do with him—training exercises, teaching tricks, trips out in the car, or going for new, interesting walks—all are equally appreciated, and will give your Miniature Schnauzer something to do and use up his physical and mental energy.

Other considerations

Now that you have decided that a Miniature Schnauzer is the dog for you, you can narrow your choice so you know exactly what you are looking for.

Male or female?

This decision really comes down to personal preference. In terms of size, there is little to choose between them; males may be slightly larger, but both sexes are within the same height range.

A female Mini Schnauzer tends to look more feminine, so if you want a slightly more distinguished head, a male may be a better option. But most pet owners are more concerned about temperament, and rightly so. Both male and female Miniature Schnauzers are affectionate and fun-loving.

Rehoming a Rescued Dog

We are fortunate that the number of Miniature Schnauzers who end up with rescue groups is relatively small. This is usually through no fault of the dog. The reasons are various, ranging from illness or death of the original owner to family breakdown, changing jobs, or even the arrival of a new baby.

It is unlikely that you will find a Mini Schnauzer in an all-breed shelter, but the breed clubs run rescue groups, and this will be your best option if you want a rescued dog.

Try to find out as much as you can about a dog's history, so you know exactly what you are taking on. You need to be realistic about what you are capable of achieving, so you can be sure you can give the dog a permanent home.

You'll need to give a rescued Miniature Schnauzer plenty of time and patience as he settles into his new home. But if all goes well, you will have the reward of knowing that you have given your dog a second chance at a forever home.

Some owners think females are better, but owners of males would swear the opposite! The only certainty is that all dogs are individuals, and you can never truly know how your dog is going to turn out.

You may find a female slightly more difficult to care for because you will need to cope with her seasonal cycle, which will start at around seven to eight months of age, with heat seasons occurring twice a year thereafter. During the three-week period of a season, you will need to keep your female away from intact males (males who have not been neutered) to eliminate the risk of pregnancy.

Many pet owners decide to spay their female, which puts an end to the seasons and also has many attendant health benefits. The operation is usually done at about six months of age. The best plan is to seek advice from your veterinarian.

An intact male may not cause many problems, although some do have a stronger tendency to mark, which could include inside the house. However, training will usually put a stop to this. An intact male will also be on the lookout for females in season, and this may lead to difficulties, depending on your circumstances.

Neutering (castrating) a male is a relatively simple operation, and there are associated health benefits. Again, you should seek advice from your veterinarian.

More than one?

Miniature Schnauzers are sociable dogs and certainly enjoy one another's company. But it's not wise to get two puppies of similar ages, or two from the same litter—no matter how tempting!

Unfortunately, there are some unscrupulous breeders who encourage people to do this, but they are thinking purely in terms of profit and not considering the welfare of the puppies.

Looking after one puppy is hard work, but taking on two pups at the same time is more than double the workload. House-training is a nightmare, as often you don't even know which puppy is making mistakes, and training is impossible unless you separate the two puppies and give them one-on-one attention.

The puppies will never be bored, because they have each other to play with. However, the likelihood is that the pair

will form a close bond, and you will come in a poor second.

If you do decide to add to your Mini Schnauzer population, wait at least 18 months, until your first dog is fully trained and grown up, before taking on another puppy.

An adult dog

You may decide to miss out on the puppy phase and get an adult dog instead. Such a dog may be harder to track down, but sometimes a breeder may have a youngster who is not suitable for showing, but is perfect for a family pet. The breeder may have kept a promising puppy, but the pup just didn't turn out as expected. Such dogs are typically well trained and well socialized by the time the breeder decides to let them go, and make great companions.

In some cases, a breeder may rehome a female when her breeding career is at an end, so she will enjoy the benefits of more individual attention. Or they may decide to let a retired show dog be pampered in a pet home.

There are advantages to taking on an adult dog, as you know exactly what you are getting. But the upheaval of changing homes can be quite upsetting, so you will need to have plenty of patience during the settling-in period.

Chapter 4

Finding Your Puppy

Your aim is to find a healthy Miniature Schnauzer puppy who has been bred and reared with the greatest possible care. Where do you begin?

One way is to attend a dog show where Miniature Schnauzers are being exhibited. The classes are divided between males and females and by ages, so you will see puppies from as young as six months, veterans, and everything in between. You will be able to see a wide range of colors and markings and, if you look closely, you will also see there are differences in type. They are all purebred Miniature Schnauzers, but breeders produce dogs with a family likeness, so you can see which type you prefer.

When the judging is finished, talk to the exhibitors and find out more about their dogs. They may not have puppies available, but some will be planning a litter, and you may decide to put your name on a waiting list.

Internet research

The Internet is an excellent resource, but when it comes to finding a puppy, use it with care.

Do go to the websites of both the American Kennel Club (AKC) and the United Kennel Club (UKC), which will give you information about the Miniature Schnauzer as a breed, and what to look for when choosing a puppy. You will also find contact details for breed clubs.

Both sites may have lists of breeders, and you can look for breeders of merit from the AKC, which indicates that a code of conduct has been followed.

Do go to the sites of the national and local breed clubs. On breed club websites you will find lots of useful information that will help you to care for your Miniature Schnauzer. There may be contact details of breeders in your area. Some websites also have a list of breeders who have puppies available. The advantage of going through a breed club is that members will follow a code of ethics, and this will give you some guarantees regarding the puppy's parents and health checks.

If you are planning to show your Miniature Schnauzer, you will need to find a breeder that specializes in show lines and has a reputation for producing top-quality dogs.

Remember that health and temperament are top priorities, so do not overlook these considerations when you are researching pedigrees.

Do not look at puppies for sale. There are legitimate Miniature Schnauzer breeders with their own websites, and they may, occasionally, advertise a litter, although in most cases reputable breeders have waiting lists for their puppies before they are even born.

The danger comes from unscrupulous breeders who produce puppies purely for profit, with no thought for the health of the dogs they breed and no care given to rearing the litter.

Photos of puppies are hard to resist, but never make a decision

based purely on an online advertisement. You need to find out who the breeder is, and have the opportunity to visit their premises and inspect the litter before making a decision.

Responsible breeders

Responsible breeders raise their puppies at home and underfoot. They have one or, at the most, two litters at a time. They carefully study the pedigrees of the male and female before they arrange any breeding, with an eye toward breeding the healthiest, most temperamentally sound dogs. Responsible breeders belong to a breed club and are involved in their breed.

Responsible breeders register their puppies with a well-estab-

lished registry such as the AKC or the UKC. (Registration with a well-established kennel club is a guarantee that your Miniature Schnauzer is truly a Miniature Schnauzer, but it is not a guarantee of good health or temperament.) They are able to hand over registration documents at the time of sale. Their breeding dogs are permanently identified by microchip or DNA. They screen them for hereditary health problems, and can tell you exactly which screening tests their dogs have had and what the results were.

You should be able to meet the mother and see where the puppies are kept. Everything should look and smell clean and healthy. The mother should be a well-socialized dog. She may be a little protective of her babies, but she should act like a typical Miniature Schnauzer.

Responsible breeders socialize all their puppies in a home environment. They provide written advice on feeding, ongoing training, socialization, parasite control, and vaccinations. They are available for phone calls after you buy their puppies, and will take a dog back at any time. They have a written contract of sale for each puppy that conforms to your state's laws.

Questions, questions, questions

When you find a responsible breeder with puppies available, you will have lots of questions to ask. These should include:

• Where have the puppies been reared? Hopefully, they will be in a home environment, which gives them the best possible start in life.

• How many males and females are in the litter?

• How many have already been spoken for? The breeder will probably be keeping a puppy to show or for breeding, and there may be other people on a waiting list.

- Can I see the mother with her puppies?
- What age are the puppies now?
- When will they be ready to go to their new homes?

Bear in mind that puppies need to be with their mother and siblings until they are a minimum of 10 weeks of age. Otherwise they miss out on vital learning and communication skills, which will have a detrimental effect on them for the rest of their lives.

The breeder should also have lots and lots of questions for you. Don't be offended! They take seriously their responsibility for every puppy they produce, and that's a good thing.

You will be asked some or all of the following questions:

- What is your home setup?
- Do you have children or grandchildren? What are their ages?
- Is there somebody at home most of the time?
- What is your previous experience with dogs?
- Do you already have other dogs at home?
- Do you want to show your Miniature Schnauzer or compete with her in one of the canine sports?

The breeder is not being intrusive; they need to understand the type of home you will provide so they can make the right match. The breeder is doing it for both the dog's benefit and also for yours.

Steer clear of a breeder who does not ask you questions. He or she may be more interested in making money from the puppies than ensuring that they go to good homes. They may also have taken other shortcuts, which may prove disastrous, and very expensive, in terms of vet bills and heartache.

Like all purebred dogs, Miniature Schnauzers have a predisposition to some health disorders, which may or may not be inherited. Ask the breeder for a full history of the parents and preceding generations to see if there are any problems you need to be aware of. Ask to see health clearances as well (more about this in Chapter 9).

Puppy watching

Puppies are irresistible, and Miniature Schnauzer pups are no exception. When you look at a litter you will be entranced; each pup has her own very individual character. But this is a situation where you must not let your heart rule your head. Always remember that you are making a long-term commitment, so you need to be 100 percent confident that the breeding stock is healthy, and the puppies have been reared with love and care.

It is a good idea to have a mental checklist of what to look for when you visit a breeder. You want to see:

- A clean, hygienic environment.
- Puppies who are outgoing, friendly, and eager to meet you.
- A sweet-natured mother who is ready to show off her puppies.
- Pups who are well-fleshed-out but not pot-bellied (which could be an indication of worms).
- Bright eyes, with no sign of soreness or discharge.
- Clean ears that smell fresh.
- No discharge from the eyes or nose.
- Clean rear ends—matting could indicate upset tummies.
- Lively pups who are keen to play.

It is important to see the mother with her puppies, as this will give you a good idea of the temperament they are likely to inherit. It is also helpful if you can see other close relatives, so you can assess the type and temperament of the dogs the breeder produces.

In most cases, you will not be

able to see the father (sire) as most breeders will travel some distance to find a stud dog who is not too close to their own bloodlines and complements their bitch. However, you should see photos of him and examine his pedigree, which will help you to make an informed decision.

Companion puppy

If you are looking for a Miniature Schnauzer as a companion, you should be guided by the breeder, who will have spent hours and hours puppy watching, and will know each of the pups as individuals. Their choice will be based on years of matchmaking experience.

It is tempting to choose a puppy yourself, but the breeder will take into account your family setup and lifestyle and will help you to pick the most suitable puppy.

Show puppy

If you are buying a puppy with the hope of showing her, make this clear to the breeder. A lot of planning goes into producing a litter, and although all the puppies will have been reared with equal care, there will be one or two who have show potential.

Ideally, recruit a breed expert to inspect the puppies with you, so you have the benefit of an objective evaluation. The breeder will also help with your choice, as they will want to ensure that only the best of their dogs are exhibited in the show ring.

Look for a puppy with the following attributes:

- A well-balanced, square body, where the length of the body equals the height at the shoulders.
- The depth of the body should equal the length of the leg.
- The head should be brick-shaped.
- The eyes must be dark, and the lips, nose, and paw pads should be black.
- The top jaw should be slightly more forward than the lower jaw so, as the pup develops, he will acquire the correct scissors bite—although this cannot be guaranteed to remain correct when the adult teeth come in.
- A tail that is set high on the back.
- Signs of a harsh coat growing under the puppy coat.
- When trotting, the legs should move in a straight line.
- A temperament that is extroverted and outgoing.

Things like color and coat texture are unimportant for a companion dog, but correct structure and bite and temperament are important for every dog.

It is easier to choose a Mini Schnauzer show puppy than many other breeds, because what you see at eight weeks is generally what you will get as an adult. However, there are no guarantees, and if your Mini Schnauzer doesn't do well in the show ring, she will still be a great companion and a much-loved member of your family.

Chapter 5

A Mini Schnauzer-Friendly Home

I t may seem like forever before your puppy is ready to leave the breeder and come home with you. But you can fill the time by getting your home ready and buying the equipment you will need. These preparations apply to a new puppy but, in reality, they are the way you will create an environment that is safe and secure for your Miniature Schnauzer throughout his life.

In the home

The Miniature Schnauzer is always alert, on the lookout for anything that appears new and interesting. If you add in a puppy's natural curiosity, you will see that your house is one big playground. Of course, you want your puppy to have fun, but the top priority is to keep him safe.

The best plan is to decide which rooms your Mini Schnauzer will have access to, and make these areas puppy friendly. Look around and ask yourself what mischief a puppy could get up to and what he could chew. Electric cords are prime candidates, so these should be safely secured where a puppy cannot reach them. Try running exposed cords and cables through PVC pipe to keep little teeth away. Anything breakable, such as glass or china, is very dangerous—once broken by a wagging tail, a puppy could step on sharp pieces or even swallow them. Houseplants also need to be out of reach, as, even if they are not poisonous, they will very likely upset a puppy's tummy.

Make sure all cupboards and storage units cannot be opened—or broken into, especially in the kitchen and bathroom, where you may store cleaning materials and other substances that are toxic to dogs.

If you have stairs, it would be wise to declare upstairs off-limits. Negotiating stairs can be hazardous and puts unnecessary stress on a puppy's growing joints. The best way to do this is to put a baby gate at the bottom of the stairs—but make sure your puppy can't squeeze through it or under it when he is very small.

In the yard

The Miniature Schnauzer is not a big dog, but he is surprisingly agile, so you need to check that all fencing is secure and high enough. The Mini Schnauzer is not a great escape artist; he sees his role as a watchdog, patrolling the boundaries, but it is better to be safe than sorry. Gates need to be sturdy with a good latch that cannot be opened by an intelligent and determined dog.

Be aware of chemicals you may have in your yard, such as fertilizer for the lawn, or weed or bug killer. Any of these, if eaten by a dog, could be fatal. Keep all toxic substances in a secure place, well out of reach. Rat poison, slug pellets, and antifreeze are particularly dangerous. Find out if your garden contains plants that are poisonous to dogs. There is not enough room to list them all here, but you can find a full list at www.aspca.org/pet-care/animal-poison-control/toxic-and-non-toxic-plants.

Swimming pools and ponds should be covered, as most puppies are fearless, and although it is easy for a puppy to take the plunge, it is virtually impossible for him to get out unaided.

You will also need to designate a toileting area. This will help with the housetraining process, and it will also make cleaning up easier.

House rules

Before your puppy comes home, hold a family conference to decide on the house rules. For example, is your Mini Schnauzer going to be allowed to roam freely, or will you keep him in the kitchen unless you can supervise him elsewhere? When you're on the sofa, is he allowed to come on your lap for a cuddle? These are personal choices, but once you have let your puppy do something, he will think this is allowed, regardless of whether you change your mind.

The most important thing is to be consistent. You and your family must make decisions, and stick with them. Otherwise your puppy will be upset and confused, not understanding what you want of him.

Going shopping

There are some essential items you will need for your Miniature Schnauzer. If you choose wisely, much of it will last for many years to come.

Indoor crate

Rearing a puppy is so much easier if you invest in an indoor crate. It provides a safe haven for your puppy at night, when you have to go out during the day, and at other times when you cannot supervise him. A puppy needs a base where he feels safe and secure, and where he can rest undisturbed. An indoor crate provides the perfect den, and many adult dogs continue to use them throughout

their lives. You need to buy a crate that will be big enough to accommodate your Miniature Schnauzer when he is fully grown. He must be able to stand up and turn around.

You will also need to think about where you are going to put the crate. The kitchen is often the most suitable place, as this is the hub of family life. Find a snug corner where the puppy can rest when he wants to, but where he can also see what is going on around him and still be with the family.

Collar and leash

You may think that it is not worth buying a collar for the first few weeks, but the sooner your pup gets used to it, the better. All you need is a lightweight nylon baby collar; you can buy something more exotic when your Mini Schnauzer is fully grown.

A nylon leash is suitable for early training, but make sure the fastening is secure. Again, you can invest in a more expensive leash at a later date—there are lots of attractive collar and leash sets to choose from.

Beds and bedding

The crate will need to be lined with bedding, and the best type to buy is synthetic fleece. This is warm and cozy, and because moisture soaks through it, your puppy will not have a wet bed when he is tiny and is still unable to go through the night without relieving himself.

Fleece is machine washable and easy to dry; buy two pieces, so you have one to use while the other is in the wash.

If you have purchased a crate, you may not feel the need to buy an extra bed, although many Mini Schnauzers like to have a bed in the family room so they feel part of household activities. There is an amazing array of dog beds to chose from—bean bags, cushions, baskets, igloos, mini-four posters—so you can take your pick! Before you make a major investment, wait until your puppy has gone through the chewing phase; you will be surprised at how much damage can be inflicted by small teeth.

ID

Your Miniature Schnauzer needs to wear some form of ID when he is out in public. This can be a tag engraved with your contact details and attached to the collar. When your Miniature Schnauzer is full-grown, you can buy an embroidered collar with your contact

details, which eliminates the danger of the tag falling off.

You may also wish to consider a permanent form of ID. Increasingly, breeders are getting puppies microchipped before they go to their new homes. A microchip is the size of a grain of rice. It is injected under the skin, usually between the shoulder blades, with a special needle.

Each chip has its own unique identification number that can only be read by a special scanner. That ID number is then registered on a national database with your name and details, so if your dog is lost, any veterinarian or shelter where he is scanned can contact you. If your puppy has not been microchipped, you can ask your vet to do it, maybe when he goes in for his vaccinations.

Bowls

Your Miniature Schnauzer will need two bowls; one for food, and one for fresh drinking water, which should always be readily available. A stainless steel bowl is a good choice for a food bowl. Plastic bowls will almost certainly be chewed, and there is a danger that bacteria can collect in the small cracks that may appear. You can get a second stainless steel bowl for drinking water, or you may prefer a heavier ceramic bowl, which will not be knocked over so easily.

Food

The breeder will let you know what your puppy is eating and should provide a full diet sheet to guide you through the first six months of your puppy's feeding regime—how much he is eating per meal, how many meals per day, when to increase the amounts per meal, and when to reduce the meals per day.

The breeder may provide you with some food when you pick up your puppy, but it is worth inquiring in advance about the availability of the brand that is recommended.

Grooming equipment

The Miniature Schnauzer needs extensive coat care throughout his life, and unless you go to a professional groomer, that means buying a lot of grooming equipment. To start, buy what you need for a puppy, and then invest in more equipment as you need it.

For a puppy you will need:
- A small, soft slicker brush
- A small, fine comb
- A large metal comb
- Nail clippers
- Toothbrush and toothpaste for dogs

Toys

The Miniature Schnauzer loves to play, and, as far as he is concerned, this means being a little savage with his toys. You will be surprised at how much damage puppy teeth can inflict, and adults can rip soft toys to shreds in a matter of minutes. You therefore need to provide robust toys, such as tug toys, and hard rubber Kongs, which will stand up to a Mini Schnauzer.

Get into the habit of regularly checking your dog's toys for signs of wear and tear. If your puppy swallows a chunk of rubber or plastic, it could cause an internal blockage. This could involve expensive surgery to remove it, or at worst, it could prove fatal.

Finding a veterinarian

Do this before you bring your dog home, so you have a vet to call if there is a problem. Visit some of the vets in your area, and speak to other pet owners to find out who they recommend. It is as important to find a good vet as it is to find a good doctor for yourself. You need to find someone with whom you can build a good rapport and have complete faith in. Word of mouth is really the best recommendation.

When you contact a veterinary practice, find out:

- What facilities are available at the practice?

- What are the plans for emergency and after-hours care?
- Do the vets in the practice have experience treating Mini Schnauzers?

If you are satisfied with what you find, and the staff appear to be helpful and friendly, book an appointment so your puppy can have a health check a couple of days after you bring him home. The vet will need to see the vaccination record and will record all the details both for you and the dog. He or she will discuss with you feeding, worming, parasite treatments, and probably microchipping, at the first visit.

Settling in

When you first arrive home with your puppy, be careful not to overwhelm him. You and your family are hugely excited, but the puppy is in a completely unfamiliar environment with new sounds, smells, and sights. This is a daunting experience, even for the boldest of pups.

The majority of Miniature Schnauzer puppies are very confident—exploring their new surroundings, wanting to play right away and quickly making friends. Others need a little longer to find their feet. Keep a close eye on your puppy's body language and reactions so you can proceed at a pace he is comfortable with.

First, let him explore a little bit outside. He will probably need to relieve himself after the trip home, so take him to the designated toileting area and, when he performs, give him plenty of praise.

When you take your puppy indoors, let him investigate again. Show him his crate, and encourage him to enter by throwing in a treat. Let him sniff, and allow him to go in and out as he wants. Later on, when he is tired, you can put him in the crate while you stay in the room. This way, he will learn to settle and will not think he is being abandoned.

It is a good idea to feed your puppy in his crate, at least to begin with, as this helps to build up a positive association. It will not be long before your Miniature Schnauzer sees his crate as his own special den and will go there on his own. Some owners place a blanket over the crate, covering the back and sides, so that it is even more cozy and den-like.

Meeting the family

Resist the temptation to invite friends and neighbors to come and meet the new arrival. Your puppy needs to focus on getting to know his new family for the first few days. Try not to swamp your Miniature Schnauzer with too much attention—he needs a chance to explore and find his own way. There will be plenty of time for cuddles later on!

If you have children in the family, you need to keep everything as calm as possible. Your puppy may not have met children before, and even if he has, he will still find them strange and unpredictable.

A puppy can easily become alarmed by too much noise, or he may go to the opposite extreme and become over-excited, which can lead to mouthing and nipping.

The best plan is to get the children to sit on the floor and give them each a treat. Each child can then call the puppy, pet him, and offer the treat. This way, the puppy interacts with each child calmly and sensibly to get his treat.

If he tries to nip or mouth, make sure there is a toy ready nearby, so his attention can be diverted to something he is allowed to bite. If you do this consistently, he will learn to inhibit his desire to mouth when he is interacting with people.

Right from the start, impose a rule that the children are not allowed to pick up or carry the puppy. They can cuddle him when they are sitting on the floor. This may sound a little severe, but a

wriggly puppy can be dropped in an instant, sometimes with disastrous consequences.

Involve all family members with your puppy's day-to-day care. This will develop his bond with the whole family, as opposed to just one person. Encourage the children to train and reward the puppy, so he learns to follow cues from everyone in the family.

The animal family

Miniature Schnauzers are sociable and enjoy the company of other dogs, but if you already own a dog, make sure you supervise early interactions so relations start off on the right foot.

Ideally, introduce your resident dog to the newcomer at the breeder's home. This works well because the puppy feels secure and the

adult dog does not feel threatened. But if this is not possible, allow your dog to smell the puppy's bedding (bedding supplied by the breeder is fine) before they actually meet, so he familiarizes himself with the puppy's scent.

Outdoors is the best place to introduce the puppy, since the adult will regard it as neutral territory. He will probably take a great interest in the puppy and sniff him all over. Most puppies are naturally submissive in this situation, and your pup may lick the other dog's mouth or roll over on to his back. Try not to interfere, as this is the natural way dogs get to know each other.

You will only need to intervene if the older dog is too boisterous, and alarms the puppy. In this case, it is a good idea to put the adult on his leash so you have some measure of control.

It rarely takes long for an adult to accept a puppy, since he does not constitute a threat. This will be underlined if you make a big fuss over the older dog, so he has no reason to feel jealous. However, do not take any risks and supervise all interactions for the first few weeks. If you do need to leave the dogs alone, always make sure your puppy is safe in his crate.

Meeting a cat should be supervised in a similar way, but do not allow your puppy to be rough, as the cat may retaliate using her sharp claws. A Miniature Schnauzer puppy is likely to be highly excited by the sight of a new furry friend, and will probably run up and bark at the cat. Make sure you stop this immediately, before bad habits develop.

The best way to do this is to keep distracting your puppy by calling him to you and offering him treats. This way, he will switch his focus from the cat to you, and you can reward him for his good behavior.

The most important thing you can do is make sure your cat has plenty of elevated spots in every room, well out of the puppy's reach, to which she can retreat. Feed her up high, as well, so she will not be bothered. And if the puppy is showing too much interest in her litter box, put it in a room that is blocked with a baby gate, so kitty can go over but the puppy can't get in.

Generally, the canine-feline relationship should not cause any serious problems. Indeed, many Mini Schnauzers count the family cat among their best friends!

Feeding

The breeder will generally provide enough food for the first few days, so your puppy does not have to cope with a change in diet—and possible digestive upset—along with all the stress of moving to a new home.

Some puppies eat up their food from the very first meal; others are more concerned about their new surroundings and are too distracted to eat. Don't worry if your puppy seems uninterested in his food for the first day or so. Give him 10 minutes to eat what he wants, then remove the leftovers and give him fresh food at the next meal. Do not make the mistake of trying to tempt him with tasty treats or you will end up with a picky eater. A scenario can develop where the dog holds out, refusing to eat his food, in the hope that something better will be offered.

Obviously, if you have any concerns about your puppy in the first few days, seek advice from your vet.

The first night

Your puppy will have spent his entire life so far with his mother or curled up with his siblings. He is then taken from everything he knows as familiar, lavished with attention by his new family—and then comes bedtime when he is left all alone. It is little wonder that he feels abandoned!

The best plan is to establish a nighttime routine, and then stick to it so that your puppy knows what is expected of him. Take your puppy outside to relieve himself, and then settle him in his crate. Some people leave a low light on for the puppy at night for the first week, others have tried soft music as company or a ticking clock. A covered hot-water bottle filled with warm water can also be a comfort. Like people, puppies are all individuals and what works for one, does not necessarily work for another, so it is a matter of trial and error.

Be very positive when you leave your puppy on his own. Do not linger or keep returning; this will make the situation more difficult.

It is inevitable that he will protest to begin with, but if you stick to your routine, he will accept that he gets left at night—but you always return in the morning.

Rescued dogs

Settling an older, rescued dog in your home is very similar to a puppy, and you will need to make the same preparations for his homecoming. As with a puppy, an adult dog will need you to be consistent, so start as you mean to go on.

There is often an initial honeymoon period when you bring a rescued dog home, where he will be on his best behavior for the first few weeks. It is after this period that the true nature of the dog will show, so be prepared for subtle changes in his behavior. It may be advisable to register with a reputable trainer, so you can seek advice on any training or behavioral issues at an early stage.

Above all, remember that a rescued dog ceases to be a rescued dog the moment he enters his forever home with you.

Housetraining

This is an aspect of training that most first-time puppy owners dread, but it should not be a problem as long as you are prepared to put in the time and effort.

Some breeders start the house training process by providing the litter with paper or training pads so they learn to keep their sleeping quarters clean. This is a step in the right direction, but most pet owners want their puppies to toilet outside.

You will have allocated a toileting area in your yard or somewhere else outdoors when preparing for your puppy's homecoming. Take your puppy to this area every time he needs to relieve himself so he builds up an association and knows why you have brought him outside.

Establish a routine and make sure you take your puppy out at the following times:
- First thing in the morning
- After mealtimes
- When he wakes up
- After a play session
- Last thing at night

Tips on housetraining a puppy.

A puppy should be taken out to relieve himself every two hours as an absolute minimum. If you can manage an hourly trip out, so much the better. The more often your puppy gets it right, the quicker he will learn to be clean in the house. It helps if you use a verbal cue, such as "busy," when your pup is performing, and in time, this will trigger the desired response.

Do not be tempted to put your puppy out on the doorstep to the backyard in the hope that he will toilet on his own. Most pups simply sit there, waiting to get back inside the house! No matter how bad the weather is, accompany your puppy and give him lots of praise when he performs correctly. Do not rush back inside as soon as he

has finished; your puppy might start to delay in the hope of prolonging his time outside with you. Praise him, have a quick game—and then you can both return indoors.

When accidents happen

No matter how vigilant you are, there are bound to be accidents. If your puppy has an accident, always ask yourself: Did I give him enough opportunity? What should I do differently?

If you witness the accident, take your puppy outside immediately, and give him lots of praise if he finishes his business out there. If you are not there when he has an accident, do not scold him when you discover what has happened. He will not remember what he has done and will not understand why you are angry with him. Simply clean it up and resolve to be more vigilant next time.

Make sure you use a cleaner that's made for pet urine when you clean up. Otherwise your pup will be drawn to the smell and may be tempted to use the same spot again.

Choosing a diet

There are so many different types of dog food to choose from, it can be bewildering. The priority is to find a good-quality, well-balanced diet. This is an active breed, and he'll need a diet that is suited to his individual requirements.

Dry food

Most dry foods, or kibble, are scientifically formulated to meet all your dog's nutritional needs. Kibble is certainly convenient, and is often less expensive than other diets.

Which kibble is best? This is a difficult question, and the best plan is to seek advice from your puppy's breeder or your veterinarian. Generally, an adult maintenance diet should contain 21 to 24 percent protein and 10 to 14 percent fat. Protein levels should be higher in puppy diets, and reduced in senior diets.

Kibble can be fed on its own, or along with other types of food. It is best fed in a puzzle toy—a toy dogs must manipulate in some way to get the food out. No dog is too young—or too old!—to start eating kibble from a puzzle toy.

Canned food and pouches

Canned food contains a lot more water than kibble. Some canned foods—although certainly not all—will have fewer carbohydrates than kibble. The more natural wet foods contain rice rather than other cereals containing gluten, so select this type to avoid allergic reactions. Read the label carefully so you are aware of the ingredients and, remember, what you put in will affect what comes out.

Canned food can be all or part of your dog's diet. Even if it is only a part, the label should say the diet is complete and balanced for your dog.

Homemade

There are some owners who like to prepare meals especially for their dogs—and it is probably much appreciated. The danger is that although the food is tasty, and your Miniature Schnauzer may appreciate the variety, you cannot be sure that it has the correct nutritional balance. There are a lot of raw diet recipes on the Internet, for example, but recent research has found that the majority of them do not offer complete and balanced nutrition.

Commercially prepared raw diets may come fresh or frozen or freeze-dried, or you might choose to prepare your dog's diet yourself. They typically contain raw meat, bones, organ meats, fat, vegetables, and sometimes, some cooked grains. Proponents of raw diets believe they are providing the dog with a food that is very close to the natural diet he would eat in the wild.

If you're buying a commercial raw diet, look for a statement on the label that says it's complete and balanced. If you want to prepare the diet yourself, work with a veterinary nutritionist to formulate a healthy diet for your dog.

Feeding schedule

When your puppy arrives in his new home, he will need four meals evenly spaced throughout the day. You may decide to stick with the food recommended by your puppy's breeder, and if your pup is thriving there is no need to change. However, if your puppy is not doing well on the food, or you have problems with supply, you will need to make a change.

When switching diets, it is very important to do it gradually, changing over from one food to the next a little at a time, and spreading the transition over a week to 10 days. This will avoid the risk of digestive upset.

When your puppy is around 12 weeks, you can cut out one of his meals. He may well have started to leave some of his food, indicating he is ready to do this. By six months, he can move on to two meals a day—a regime that will suit him for the rest of his life.

Bones and chews

Puppies love to chew, and many adults also enjoy gnawing on a bone. Bones should always be hard and uncooked. Never feed rib bones or poultry bones, as they can splinter and cause major problems. Dental chews, and many of the manufactured rawhide chews are safe, but they should be given only under supervision.

Ideal weight

To keep your Miniature Schnauzer in good health, you must monitor his weight. It is all too easy for the pounds to pile on, and this can result in serious health problems. The Mini Schnauzer takes food very seriously and has perfected the art of fixing you with a gaze and telling you he is "starving." You will therefore need to harden your heart and think of your dog's health! If you are using treats for training, remember to reduce the amount you feed at his next meal.

When you are assessing your dog's weight, look at him from above, and make sure you can see a definite "waist." You should be able to feel his ribs, but not see them.

To keep a check on your dog's weight, get into the habit of visiting your vet clinic once a month just to weigh your dog. You can keep a record and adjust his diet, if necessary. If you are concerned that your Miniature Schnauzer is putting on too much weight, or if you think he is underweight, consult your veterinarian, who will help you plan a suitable diet.

Chapter 6

Caring for Your Mini Schnauzer

The Miniature Schnauzer is easy to care for in terms of diet and exercise, but she is definitely high-maintenance when it comes to coat care.

Puppy grooming

A Miniature Schnauzer will spend a relatively large proportion of his life on the grooming table, so it is important that he learns to enjoy the attention. If a dog dislikes being handled, major problems can develop—so much so that he may even become aggressive when any attempt is made to groom him.

All these problems are easily avoided if your puppy gets accustomed to being groomed and handled from an early age. In fact, many dogs positively enjoy grooming sessions, viewing them as quality time spent with their people.

The first task is to teach your puppy to stand on a table. It does not have to be an actual grooming table—just one that is steady and

is the right height for you to attend to your Mini Schnauzer without getting a backache. Place a rubber mat on the table so your puppy does not slip and, to start with, let her sit or stand while you stroke her and praise her for being calm. Reward her with a treat, and that will be enough for the first session.

The next day, you can use a slicker bush to groom her for a few minutes. The breeder will have introduced grooming, so once your puppy feels confident with you, she should start to relax. You will then need to comb through the longer hair (furnishings) on the legs and hindquarters and the beard. A wide-toothed metal comb is best for this job, then use a small, fine-toothed comb for the eyebrows. When your puppy first arrives home, she will not have much in the way of furnishings, but it is important that she gets used to the procedure.

Adult grooming

The Miniature Schnauzer's adult coat consists of a soft but dense undercoat and a harsh, wiry topcoat. You will find it much easier to allocate a few minutes every day to grooming, rather than neglecting the coat and only grooming when it becomes matted and tangled.

As with a puppy, you will need to work though the body coat with a slicker brush, and then comb through the furnishings, teasing out any knots. As the coat grows, the beard will need daily atten-

tion because it can become soiled with food and other debris.

The beard and the skirt (the underside) will also need trimming, or else they become long and straggly, and impossible to manage. You can learn how to do this yourself, or you can have it done when your dog goes to a professional groomer to be clipped.

Bathing

There is no need to bathe your Miniature Schnauzer regularly, and too much bathing will dry out the skin and coat. Most pet owners reserve a full bath for when their dog has rolled in something particularly smelly. However, the beard and the leg furnishing should be washed once a week, using a shampoo and conditioner that is specially formulated for dogs.

Accustom your puppy
to grooming from an
early stage.

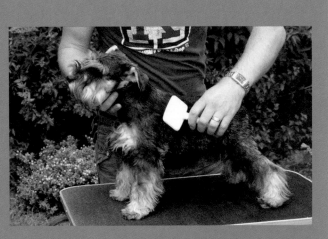

The workload
increases as the adult
coat comes in

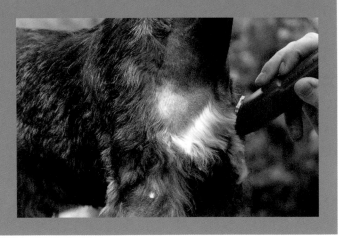

Pet dogs are
generally trimmed
close to the body.

Clipping

Most owners of pet Miniature Schnauzers maintain the coat by having it clipped. This looks very smart and certainly cuts down on the huge workload associated with hand stripping and scissoring.

On average, your Miniature Schnauzer will need to be clipped by a professional groomer every six weeks. This involves clipping the top of the head, cheeks, throat, chest, and body.

Show presentation

There is nothing wrong with having your pet Miniature Schnauzer clipped—indeed, it is the best way of caring for his coat. However, it will not do for a show dog. The process of clipping destroys the harsh, wiry texture of the coat, so show dogs must be hand-stripped.

This is a laborious process, which involves pulling out the dead hair with finger and thumb. All areas are stripped, except for the cheeks, throat, ears, underside, and rear, which are clipped. The legs, eyebrows, and beard are scissored.

Most people with show dogs work on the coat every day, gradually enhancing the shape so the dog looks her best in the show ring. There is a huge amount of skill involved—as well as a lot of expensive grooming equipment—so it is definitely a job for the professionals.

Show dogs need to have their coat stripped, using a stripping knife or finger and thumb.

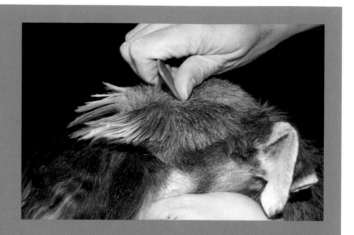

The cheeks, throat, underside, and ears are clipped..

The longer furnishings are timmerd with scissors.

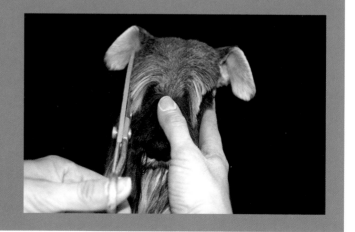

Routine care

In addition to grooming, your dog will need some routine care.

Eyes

Check the eyes for signs of soreness or discharge. You can use a separate piece of cotton for each eye, and wipe away any debris.

Ears

The ears should be clean and free from odor. You can buy specially manufactured ear wipes, or you can use a piece of cotton to clean them, if necessary. Do not probe into the ear canal or you risk doing more harm than good.

You will also need to pluck the hair that grows inside the ears. This is most easily done using finger and thumb, or you can use blunt tweezers. The process is easier if you use an ear powder; the hair comes out more easily and causes less distress. Start doing this from an early age, rewarding your puppy for her cooperation, so she learns to accept it without a fuss.

Teeth

Dental disease is becoming more prevalent among dogs so teeth cleaning should be an essential part of your care regime. The build- up of tartar on the teeth can result in tooth decay, gum infection, and bad breath, and if it is allowed to accumulate, you may have no option but to get the teeth cleaned under anesthesia.

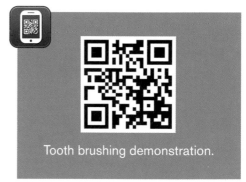

Tooth brushing demonstration.

When your Miniature Schnauzer is still a puppy, get her used to teeth cleaning so it becomes a matter of routine. Dog toothpaste comes in a variety of meaty flavors, which your Mini Schnauzer will like, so you can start by putting some toothpaste on your finger and gently rubbing her teeth. You can then progress to using a finger brush or a toothbrush, whichever you find most convenient.

Remember to reward your Miniature Schnauzer when she cooperates and then she will positively look forward to her teeth-cleaning sessions.

Nails

Nail trimming is a task dreaded by many owners—and many dogs—but again, if you start early, your Miniature Schnauzer will get used to the procedure.

Dark nails are harder to trim than white nails because you cannot see the quick (the vein and nerves that run through the nail) and it will bleed if it is nicked. The best policy is to trim little and often so the nails don't grow too long, and you do not risk cutting too much and nicking the quick.

If you are worried about trimming your Mini Schnauzer's nails, go to your vet so you can see it done properly. If you are still concerned, you can always use the services of a professional groomer.

Exercise

The Miniature Schnauzer is lively and energetic and will need regular, varied exercise. Going for walks gives a dog the opportunity to use her nose and investigate new sights and smells, and even if she does not walk for miles, she will appreciate going to new places. The Mini Schnauzer has an excellent sense of smell, and an opportunity to explore new places will be viewed as a great treat.

If, for any reason, your time is limited, it is useful if you can teach your Mini Schnauzer to retrieve a toy. She will expend a lot of energy playing this game and will also enjoy the mental stimulation.

If you have more than one dog, they will burn off a lot of energy playing together. If you have a lone dog, why not find a dog-walking friend (as long as their dog is of sound temperament) and you can all enjoy a sociable time together.

The older Mini Schnauzer

We are fortunate that the Miniature Schnauzer has a good life expectancy, and you will not notice any significant changes in your dog until she reaches double figures, or maybe even later.

The older Mini Schnauzer will sleep more, and she may be reluctant to go for longer walks. She may show signs of stiffness when she gets up from her bed, but these generally ease when she starts moving. Some older Miniature Schnauzers may have impaired vision, and some may become a little deaf, but as long as their senses do not deteriorate dramatically, this is something older dogs learn to live with.

If you treat your older Mini Schnauzer with kindness and consideration, she will enjoy her later years and suffer a minimum of discomfort. It is advisable to switch her over to a senior diet, which is more suited to her needs, and you may need to adjust the quantity, as she will not be burning up the calories she did when she was younger and more energetic. Make sure her sleeping quarters are warm and free from drafts, and if she gets wet, make sure you dry her thoroughly.

Most important of all, be guided by your Miniature Schnauzer. She will have good days when she feels up to going for a walk, and other days when she would prefer to putter around at home. If you have a younger dog, this may well stimulate your Mini Schnauzer to take more of an interest in what is going on, but make sure she is not pestered, as she needs to rest undisturbed when she is tired.

Letting go

Inevitably there comes a time when your Miniature Schnauzer is not enjoying a good quality of life, and you need to make the painful decision to let her go. We all wish that our dogs died painlessly in their sleep, but unfortunately, this is rarely the case.

However, we can allow our dogs to die with dignity, and to suffer as a little as possible, and this should be our way of saying thank you for the wonderful companionship they have given us.

When you feel the time is drawing near, talk to your veterinarian, who will be able to make an objective assessment of your Mini Schnauzer's condition and will help you to make the right decision.

This is the hardest thing you will ever have to do as a dog owner, and it is only natural to grieve for your beloved Mini Schnauzer. But eventually, you will be able to look back on the happy memories of times spent together, and this will bring much comfort. You may, in time, feel that your life is not complete without a Miniature Schnauzer, and you will feel ready to welcome a new dog into your home.

Chapter 7

Training Your Mini Schnauzer

To live in the modern world without fear and anxieties, a Mini Schnauzer needs an education in social skills, so that he learns to cope calmly and confidently in a wide variety of situations.

Early learning

The breeder will have begun a program of socialization by getting the puppies used to all the sights and sounds of a busy household. You need to continue this when your pup arrives in his new home, making sure he is not worried by household appliances, such as the vacuum cleaner and the washing machine, and that he gets used to unexpected noises from the stereo and television.

It is important to handle your puppy regularly so he will accept grooming and other routine care, and will not be worried if he has to be examined by the veterinarian.

To begin with, your puppy needs to get used to all the members

of his new family, but then you should give him the opportunity to meet friends and other people who come to the house.

Miniature Schnauzers are natural watchdogs, and while a warning bark is acceptable, you do not want your dog to continue barking at visitors. Right from the start, teach him acceptable greeting behavior in the following way:

- Have some treats ready, and once your puppy has said his first hello, distract his attention by calling him to you, giving him a treat, and praising him for coming to you.
- Let him return to the visitor (hopefully, not barking), and then call him back to you for a treat and praise. In this way, the pup learns that coming to you is more rewarding than making a fuss about a visitor.
- Now give the visitor a couple of treats so that when your puppy approaches—and is not barking—he can be rewarded. Remember, only reward when the dog is not barking.

This training may take a bit of practice, but it is well worth the effort.

It is also very important that your puppy learns to interact with children. If you do not have children of your own, make sure your puppy has the chance to meet and play with other people's children—making sure interactions are always supervised—so he learns that humans come in small sizes too.

The outside world

When your puppy has completed his vaccinations, he is ready to venture into the wider world. Mini Schnauzer puppies take a lively interest in everything new. However, there is a lot for a small puppy to take in, so do not swamp him with too many new experiences when you first set out.

And of course, you need to work on leash training before you go on your first expedition. There will be plenty of distractions to deal with, so you do not want additional problems of coping with a dog who is pulling or lagging on the leash. Spend some time training, and you can set off with your Mini Schnauzer walking by your side on a loose leash.

He may need additional encouragement when you venture farther afield, so arm yourself with some extra special treats, which will give him a good reason to focus on you when you need him to.

Start by walking your puppy in a quiet area with light traffic, and only progress to a busier place when he is ready. There is so much to see and hear—people (maybe carrying bags or umbrellas), strollers, bicycles, cars, trucks, machinery—so give your puppy a chance to take it all in.

If he does appear worried, do not fall into the trap of sympathizing with him, or worse still, picking him up. This will only teach your pup that he had a good reason to be worried and, with luck, you will "rescue" him if he feels scared.

Instead, give him a little space so he does not have to confront whatever he is frightened of, and distract him with a few treats. Then ask him to walk past, using an encouraging tone of voice, never forcing him by yanking on the leash. Reward him for any forward movement, and your puppy will soon learn that he can trust you and there is nothing to fear.

Dog to dog meetings

Your pup also needs to continue his education in canine manners, which was started by his mother and by his littermates, as he must be able to greet all dogs calmly, giving the signals that say he is friendly.

Find a friend who has a dog with a solid temperament and visit their house. Allow the two dogs to play outside for 10 minutes or so. Do not prolong the game, as you do not want your youngster to become over-excited or overwhelmed.

Once the two dogs have had a few playdates at home, go for a walk and allow them to exercise together off leash. They will interact with each other, but their focus will shift periodically as they will be distracted by other sights and smells.

Extend your Mini Schnauzer's circle of acquaintances by finding other friends who have dogs of sound temperament, ideally representing a number of different breeds, sizes, and types.

The more your Mini Schnauzer practices meeting and greeting, the better he will become at reading body language and assessing other dogs' intentions.

Training classes

A training class will give your Mini Schnauzer the opportunity to work alongside other dogs in a controlled situation, and he will also learn to focus on you in a different, distracting environment. Both these lessons will be vital as your dog matures.

However, the training class needs to be well run, or you risk doing more harm than good. Before you go along with your puppy, attend a class as an observer to make sure you are happy with what goes on. Find out:

- How much training experience do the instructors have?
- Are the classes divided into appropriate ages and sizes?
- Do they use positive, reward-based training methods?
- Do any of the instructors have experience with Mini Schnauzers?

If the training class is well run, it is certainly worth attending. Both you and your Mini Schnauzer will learn useful training exercises. It will increase his social skills, and you will have the chance to talk to lots of like-minded dog lovers.

Training guidelines

The Miniature Schnauzer is a highly intelligent dog and is generally eager to please. However, he is a smart dog with his own ideas, so training is important.

You will be keen to get started, but in your rush to get training underway, do not forget the fundamentals that could make the difference between success and failure. You need to get into the mindset of a Mini Schnauzer, figuring out what motivates him and, equally, what makes him switch off. Decide on your priorities for training, set realistic goals, and then think of ways to make your training positive and rewarding.

When you start training, try to observe the following guidelines:

- Choose an area that is free from distractions so your puppy will focus on you. You can progress to a more challenging environment as your pup progresses.
- Do not train your puppy just after he has eaten or exercised. He will either be too full, or too tired, to concentrate.
- Do not train if you are in a bad mood, or if you are short of time—these sessions always end in disaster!
- Providing a worthwhile reward is an essential tool in training. You will probably get the best results if you use some extra special food treats, although some Mini Schnauzers get very focused on toys, and will see a game with a favorite toy as a top reward.
- If you decide to use a toy, make sure it is only brought out for training sessions, so it accrues added value.
- Keep your verbal cues simple, and always use the same one for each exercise. For example, when you ask your puppy to go into the Down position, the cue is "Down," not "Lie Down," "Get Down," or anything else. Remember, your Mini Schnauzer does not speak English; he associates the sound of the word with the action.
- If your dog is finding an exercise difficult, break it down into smaller steps so it is easier to understand.
- Do not make your training sessions boring and repetitious. If training is dull, your puppy will lose focus and go off to find something more interesting to do.
- Do not train for too long, particularly with a young puppy, who has a very short attention span.
- Always end training sessions on a positive note. This does not necessarily mean getting an exercise right. If your pup is

tired and making mistakes, ask him to do a simple exercise so you have the opportunity to praise and reward him. You may find that he benefits from having a break and will make better progress next time you try.

Remember that if your Mini Schnauzer is rewarded for a behavior, he is likely to repeat it—so make sure you are 100 percent consistent and always reward the behavior you want to see.

First lessons

Like all puppies, a young Mini Schnauzer will soak up new experiences like a sponge, so training should start from the time your pup arrives in his new home. It is much easier to teach good habits than trying to correct your puppy when he has established an undesirable pattern of behavior.

Wearing a collar

Even if he doesn't wear a collar in the house, he will be on a leash when he goes out in public places, so he needs to get used to the feel of a collar around his neck. Some puppies think nothing of wearing a collar, while others act as if they are being strangled! It is best to accustom your pup to wearing a soft collar for a few minutes at a time, until he gets used to it.

Fit the collar so that you can get at least two fingers between the collar and his neck. Then have a game to distract his attention. This will work for a few moments. Then he will stop and start scratching away at the peculiar thing around his neck. Bend down, rotate the collar, pat him on the head, and distract him by playing with a toy or giving him a treat.

After he has worn the collar for a few minutes each day, he will soon ignore it. Remember, never leave the collar on the puppy unsu-

pervised, especially when he is outside in the yard, or when he is in his crate, as it is could get snagged, causing serious injury.

Walking on the leash

Inside info on Mini Schnauzers

Once your puppy is used to the collar, take him outside into a secure area, such as your backyard, where there are no distractions. Attach the leash and, to begin with, allow him to wander with the leash trailing, making sure it does not become snagged. Then pick up the leash and follow the pup where he wants to go; he needs to get used to the sensation of being attached to you.

The next stage is to get your Mini Schnauzer to follow you, and for this you will need some treats. To give yourself the best chance of success, make sure the treats are high value, so your Mini Schnauzer is motivated to work with you.

Show him you have a treat in your hand, and then encourage him to follow you. Walk a few paces, and if he is walking with you, stop and reward him. If he puts on the brakes, simply change direction and lure him with the treat.

Next, introduce some changes of direction so your puppy is walking confidently alongside you. At this stage, introduce the verbal cue "Heel" when your puppy is in the correct position. You can then graduate to walking your puppy away from home, starting in quiet areas and building up to busier environments.

Do not expect too much of your puppy too soon when you are leash walking away from home. He will be distracted by all the new sights and sounds, so concentrating on leash training will be difficult for him. Give him a chance to look and see, and reward him frequently when he is walking forward confidently on a loose leash.

Come when called

Teaching a reliable recall is invaluable for both you and your Mini Schnauzer. You are secure in the knowledge that he will come back when he is called, and your Mini Schnauzer benefits from being allowed off the leash, so he has the freedom to investigate all the exciting new scents he comes across.

The Miniature Schnauzer likes to be with his people, but he also likes to explore his surroundings, and pick up on the local news by using his sense of smell. These are the times when a Mini Schnauzer may become selectively "deaf" to your calls, and is only ready to hear you when he has finished his investigations. Obviously, you can allow him a little leeway, but you do want a dog who will come when he is called.

Hopefully, the breeder will have started this lesson by calling the puppies to "Come" when it is dinnertime, or when they are moving from one place to another. You can build on this when your puppy arrives in your home, calling him to "Come" when he is in a confined space, such as the kitchen. This is a good place to build up a positive association with the verbal cue—particularly if you ask your puppy to "Come" to get his dinner!

The next stage is to transfer the lesson to a secure outdoor space, such as your backyard. Arm yourself with some treats, and wait until your puppy is distracted. Then call him, using a higher-pitched, excited tone of voice. At this stage, a puppy wants to be with you, so capitalize on this and keep practicing the verbal cue, and rewarding your puppy with a treat and lots of praise when he comes, so he knows it is worth his while to come to you.

Now you are ready to introduce some distractions. Try calling him when someone else is in the yard, or wait a few minutes until he is investigating a really interesting scent. If your puppy responds, immediately reward him with a treat. If he is slow to come, run away a few steps and then call again, making yourself sound really exciting. Jump up and down, open your arms wide to welcome him; it doesn't matter how silly you look, he needs to see you as the most fun person in the world.

When you have a reliable recall in the yard, you can venture into the outside world. Do not be too ambitious to begin with; try a recall in a quiet place with the minimum of distractions so you can be assured of success.

Do not make the mistake of asking your dog to come only at the end of his off-leash exercise or time in the yard. What is the incentive in coming back to you if all you do is clip on his leash, marking the end of his free time? Instead, call your dog at random times, giving him a treat and a pat, and then letting him go free again. This way, he learns coming to you—and focusing on you—is always rewarding.

Stationary exercises

The Sit and Down are easy to teach, and mastering these exercises will be rewarding for both you and your dog. They are useful in a wide variety of situations and mean you will always have a measure of control over your dog—for his own safety and everyone else's.

Sit

The best way to teach this cue is to lure your Mini Schnauzer into position, and for this you can use a treat or his food bowl as the reward. Hold the reward above his head and move it slightly back. As he looks up, he will lower his hindquarters and go into a sit.

Practice this a few times, and when your puppy understands what the exercise is about, introduce the verbal cue, "Sit."

When your Mini Schnauzer understands the exercise, he will respond to the verbal cue alone, and you will not need to lure or even reward him every time he sits. However, it is a good idea to give him treats at random times when he cooperates, to keep him guessing! And always reward him with praise, so he knows he's made the right choice.

Down

This is an important lesson, and can be a lifesaver if an emergency arises and you need to bring your Mini Schnauzer to an instant halt.

This is an easier exercise to teach if you start with your dog in a Sit. Stand or kneel in front of him and show him you have a treat in your hand. Hold the treat just in front of his nose and slowly lower it

Clicker Training

There are many different methods of training, and as long as the methods you use are positive and reward-based, you will not go wrong.

You may decide you want to try clicker training—a modern approach that has proved very effective. The clicker is the size of a matchbox, fitted with a small device that makes a clicking noise when it is pressed. The dog is taught that a click means a reward will follow, so he quickly learns to work for a click. The benefit is that the click enables us to mark exactly the behavior we are trying to elicit. Then, even if we're slow with the treat, the message has been delivered.

As a trainer, you need to get your timing right and click at the precise moment your dog does what you want, then reward him. This way, your dog will repeat the desired behavior, knowing that he will earn a click and then get a treat. Clicker training is easy with puppies, and adult dogs too.

toward the ground, between his front legs. As your Mini Schnauzer follows the treat, he will go down on his front legs and, in a few moments, his hindquarters will follow.

Close your hand over the treat so he doesn't cheat and get the treat before he is in the correct position. As soon as he is all the way Down, give him the treat and lots of praise. Keep practicing, and when your Mini Schnauzer understands what you want, introduce the verbal cue "Down."

Control exercises

Dogs do not always find self-control easy, and these exercises are not the most exciting. But they will make your dog much easier to live with. And he will understand that he will be rewarded for cooperating with you.

Wait

This exercise teaches your Mini Schnauzer to wait in position until you give him another cue. It differs from the Stay exercise, where he must stay where you have left him for a longer period.

The most useful application of "Wait" is when you are walking him and need him to wait at the curb, or are getting your dog out of the car and you need him to stay in position until you clip on his leash.

Start with your puppy on the leash

to give you a greater chance of success. Ask him to "Sit," then stand at his side. Take one step forward and hold your hand back behind you, palm facing the dog. Step back, release him with a word, such as "Okay," and then reward him.

Practice this a few times, waiting a little longer before you reward him, and then introduce the verbal cue "Wait." You can reinforce the lesson by using it in different situations, such as asking your Mini Schnauzer to "Wait" before you put his food bowl down.

Stay

You need to differentiate this exercise from the Wait by using a different hand signal and a different verbal cue.

Start with your Mini Schnauzer in the Down, as he is most likely to be secure in this position. Face him and take one step back, holding your hand, palm flat, facing him. Wait a second and then come back to stand in front of him.

Practice until your Mini Schnauzer understands the exercise, and then introduce the verbal cue "Stay." Gradually increase the distance between you and your puppy, and increase the challenge by walking around him—and even stepping over him—so that he learns he must "Stay" until you release him, using your release word, "Okay."

Leave

A response to this verbal cue means your Mini Schnauzer will learn to give up a toy on request, and it follows that he will give up anything when he is asked, which is very useful if he has got hold of a forbidden object such as a shoe or somebody's glove.

This is particularly important with a Mini Schnauzer, who can become possessive with favorite toys or places of high value, such as the sofa, or even your bed!

The "Leave" command can be taught quite easily when you are first playing with your puppy. As you gently take a toy from his mouth, introduce the verbal cue, "Leave," and then praise him. If he is reluctant, swap the toy for another toy or a treat. This will usually do the trick.

Do not try to pull the toy from his mouth if he refuses to give it up, as you will make the situation confrontational. Let the toy go "dead" in your hand, and then swap it for a new toy, or a really high-value treat, so this becomes the better option. The strategy is not to be confrontational but to offer him a better reward and then call him to you. Then he has not been forced to give up the thing he values; he has simply been offered something better!

Chapter 8

Keeping Your Mini Schnauzer Busy

The Miniature Schnauzer is quick-witted and highly intelligent, and if you have ambitions to try more advanced training or compete in one of the canine disciplines, she will be a willing pupil.

Canine Good Citizen

The American Kennel Club runs the Canine Good Citizen program. It promotes responsible ownership and helps you to train a well-behaved dog who will fit in with the community. The program tests your dog on basic good manners, alone and with other people and dogs around. It's excellent for all pet owners and is also an ideal starting point if you plan to compete in any other canine sport.

Competitive obedience

Competitive obedience exercises include: heel work at varying paces with dog and handler following a pattern decided by the judge, stays, recalls, retrieves, send-aways, scent discrimination, and distance control. The exercises get progressively harder as you rise in the classes.

The Miniature Schnauzer is more than capable of competing in this discipline, but make sure training is fun, and do not put too much pressure on your dog. To achieve top honors requires intensive training, as precision and accuracy are of paramount importance. However, you must guard against drilling your Mini Schnauzer, as he will quickly lose motivation.

Rally O

This is loosely based on obedience, and also has a few exercises borrowed from agility when you get to the highest levels. Handler and dog must complete a course, in the designated order, that has anywhere from 12 to 20 exercises. The course is timed and the team must finish within the time limit, but there are no bonus points for speed. The great advantage of rally O is that it is very relaxed, and anyone can compete.

Agility

Agility is basically a canine obstacle course. It is fast and furious and is great for the fitness of both handler and dog. And it can be quite addictive! The obstacles include hurdles, long jump, tire jump, tunnels (rigid and collapsible), weaving poles, an A-frame, a dog-walk, and a seesaw.

Agility is judged on the time taken to get around the course, with faults given for knocking down fences, missing obstacles, and going through the course in the wrong order.

The Miniature Schnauzer is a natural at this sport, and if you get your dog focused on the equipment, you will be amazed at his speed—and his enthusiasm!

Puppies should not be allowed to do any agility exercises that involve jumping or contact equipment until at least 12 months old. But while you are waiting, you can begin to teach your dog how to weave, introduce her to tunnels, and play around the jumps and poles so that she becomes familiar with the equipment.

Flyball

The Miniature Schnauzer is not a natural retriever, but with training he can enjoy the excitement of competing in flyball. It's a relay race with four dogs on a team. Each dog runs down a 51-foot (15.5 m) course, jumping over four hurdles on the way to a spring-loaded box. The dog trips the lever on the box, a tennis ball pops up, the dog

must catch it, and then run back over the four hurdles to the starting line. Then the next dog goes. The fastest team to have all four dogs run without errors, wins.

Earthdog, earth work, and barn hunt

The AKC (earthdog) and UKC (earth work) run trials are specifically designed to test the working ability of dogs who were bred to "go to ground" (search underground) for quarry. Burrows are located or created, and the dog must work the burrows to find the quarry, which she will indicate by barking, whining, scratching, or digging. The quarry are protected by wooden bars across the end of the tunnel so they are not endangered.

Barn hunt is a relatively new sport in which dogs locate rats (safely enclosed in aerated tubes) hidden in a maze of hay bales in a barn. It's a timed event. The Miniature Schnauzer is a highly enthusiastic competitor in all these ratting sports, and performs with distinction.

Showing

If you plan to exhibit your Miniature Schnauzer in the show ring, you will need to be a dedicated groomer—or employ the services of a professional—to ensure your dog looks her best when she is inspected by the judge. You will also need to spend time training your Mini Schnauzer to perform in the show ring. A dog who does not like being handled by the judge, or one who does not walk smartly on the leash, is never going to win top honors, even if she is a top-quality dog. To do well in the ring, a Miniature Schnauzer must have that quality that says, "Look at me!"

To prepare your dog for the busy show atmosphere, you need to work on her socialization, and then take her to ringcraft classes so you both learn what is required in the ring.

Musical freestyle

This is a relatively new discipline that is growing in popularity. Dog and handler must perform a choreographed routine to music, allowing the dog to perform an array of tricks and moves that delight the crowd. There are two categories: freestyle heeling, where the dog stays close to her handler in a variety of positions; and canine freestyle, where the dog works at a greater distance and performs some of the more spectacular moves.

A panel of judges marks the routine for choreography, accuracy, and musical interpretation. Both categories demand a huge amount of training, but Miniature Schnauzers enjoy the variety involved, and there are some who cannot resist the opportunity to show off!

Chapter 9

Health Care

We are fortunate that the Miniature Schnauzer is a healthy dog and, with good routine care, a well-balanced diet, and sufficient exercise, most will experience few health problems. However, it is your responsibility to put a program of preventive health care in place—and this should start from the moment your puppy, or adult dog, arrives in his new home.

Parasites

No matter how well you look after your Miniature Schnauzer, you will have to accept that parasites—internal and external—are ever present, and you need to take preventive action.

Internal parasites live inside your dog. These are the various worms. Most will find a home in the digestive tract, but there is also a parasite that lives in the heart. If infestation is unchecked, a dog's health will be severely jeopardized, but routine preventive treatment is simple and effective.

External parasites live on your dog's body—in his skin and fur, and sometimes in his ears.

Vaccination Program

The American Animal Hospital Association and the American Veterinary Medical Association have issued vaccination guidelines that apply to all breeds of dogs. They divide the available vaccines into two groups: core vaccines, which every dog should get, and non-core vaccines, which are optional.

Core vaccines are canine parvovirus-2, distemper, and adenovirus-2. Puppies should get vaccinated every three to four weeks between the ages of 6 and 16 weeks, with the final dose at 14 to 16 weeks of age.

If a dog older than 16 weeks is getting their first vaccine, one dose is enough. Dogs who received an initial dose at less than 16 weeks should be given a booster after one year, and then every three years or more thereafter.

Rabies is also a core vaccine. For puppies less than 16 weeks old, a single dose should be given no earlier than 12 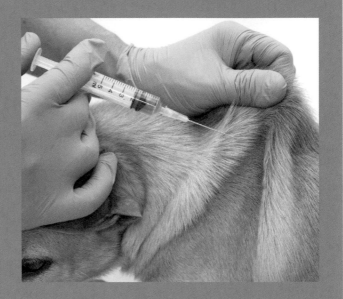 weeks of age. Revaccination is recommended annually or every three years, depending on the vaccine used and state and local laws.

Non-core vaccines are canine parainfluenza virus, Bordetella bronchiseptica, canine influenza virus, canine measles, leptospirosis, and Lyme disease.

The dog's exposure risk, lifestyle, and geographic location all come into play when deciding which non-core vaccines may be appropriate for your dog. Have a conversation with your veterinarian about the right vaccine protocol for your dog.

Roundworm

This is found in the small intestine. Signs of infestation will be a poor coat, a potbelly, diarrhea, and lethargy. Prospective mothers should be treated before mating, but it is almost inevitable that parasites she may have will be passed on to the puppies. For this reason, a breeder will start a worming program, which you will need to continue. Ask your vet for advice on treatment, which will need to continue throughout your dog's life.

Tapeworm

Infection occurs when the dog ingests fleas or lice. The adult worm takes up residence in the small intestine, releasing mobile segments (which contain eggs), which can be seen in a dog's feces as small rice-like grains. The only other obvious sign of infestation is irritation of the anus. Again, routine preventive treatment is required throughout your dog's life.

Lungworm

Lungworm is a parasite that lives in the heart and major blood vessels supplying the lungs. It can cause many problems, such as breathing difficulties, excessive bleeding, sickness, diarrhea, seizures, and even death. The dog becomes infected when ingesting slugs and snails, often accidentally when rummaging through undergrowth. Lungworm is not common, but it is on the increase and a responsible owner should be aware of it. Fortunately, it is easily preventable, and even affected dogs usually make a full recovery if treated early enough. Your vet will be able to advise you on the risks in your area and what form of treatment may be required.

Heartworm

This parasite is transmitted by mosquitoes, and is found in all parts of the USA, although its prevalence does vary. Heartworms live in the right side of the heart and larvae can grow up to 14 inches (35 cm) long. A dog with heartworm is at severe risk from heart failure, so preventive treatment, as advised by your vet, is essential. Dogs should also have regular tests to check for the presence of infection.

Fleas

A dog may carry many types of fleas. The flea stays on the dog only long enough to feed and breed, but its presence will result in itching. If your dog has an allergy to fleas—usually a reaction to the flea's saliva—he will scratch himself until he is raw. Spot-ons and chewable flea preventives are easy to use and highly effective, and should be given regularly to prevent fleas entirely. Some also prevent ticks.

If your dog has fleas, talk to your veterinarian about the best treatment. Bear in mind that your entire home, dog's whole environment, and all other pets in your home will also need to be treated.

How to Detect Fleas

You may suspect your dog has fleas, but how can you be sure? There are two methods to try. Run a fine-tooth comb through your dog's coat, and see if you can detect the presence of fleas on the skin, or clinging to the comb. Alternatively, sit your dog on some white paper and rub his back. This will dislodge feces from the fleas, which will be visible as small brown specks. To double check, shake the specks onto some damp cotton balls. Flea feces consist of the dried blood taken from the host, so if the specks turn a lighter shade of red, you know your dog has fleas.

Ticks

These are blood-sucking parasites that are most frequently found in areas

where sheep or deer are present. The main danger is their ability to pass a wide variety of very serious diseases—including Lyme disease—to both dogs and humans. The preventive you give your dog for fleas generally works for ticks, but you should discuss the best product to use with your veterinarian.

Ear mites

These parasites live in the outer ear canal. The signs of infestation are a brown, waxy discharge, and your dog will often shake his head and scratch his ear. If you suspect your dog has ear mites, a visit to the vet will be needed so that medicated ear drops can be prescribed.

Cheyletiella mange

These small, white mites are visible to the naked eye and are often referred to as "walking dandruff." They cause a scruffy coat and mild itchiness. They are zoonotic—transferable to humans—so prompt treatment with an insecticide prescribed by your veterinarian is essential.

Chiggers

These are picked up from the undergrowth, and can be seen as bright red, yellow, or orange specks on the webbing between the

How to Remove a Tick

If you spot a tick on your dog, do not try to pluck it off, as you risk leaving the hard mouth parts embedded in his skin. The best way to remove a tick is to use a pair of fine tweezers, or you can buy a tick remover. Grasp the tick head firmly and then pull the tick straight out from the skin. If you are using a tick remover, check the instructions, as some recommend a circular twist when pulling. When you have removed the tick, clean the area with mild soap and water.

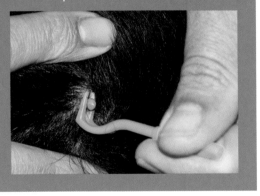

toes, although this can also be found elsewhere on the body, such as on the ear flaps. Treatment is effective with the appropriate insecticide, prescribed by your vet.

Skin mites

There are two types of parasite that burrow into a dog's skin. Demodex canis is transferred from a mother to her pups while they are feeding. Treatment is with a topical preparation, and sometimes antibiotics are needed. Refer to your vet.

The other skin mite is sarcoptes scabiei, which causes intense itching and hair loss. It is highly contagious, so all dogs in a household will need to be treated, which involves repeated bathing with a medicated shampoo.

Common ailments

As with all living animals, dogs can be affected by a variety of ailments, most of which can be treated effectively after consulting with your vet, who will prescribe appropriate medication and will advise you on how to care for your dog's needs.

Here are some of the more common problems that could affect your Miniature Schnauzer, with advice on how to deal with them.

Anal glands

These are two small sacs on either side of the anus, which produce a dark brown secretion. The anal glands should empty every time a dog defecates, but if they become blocked or impacted, a dog will experience increasing discomfort. He may lick at his rear end, or scoot his bottom along the ground to relieve the irritation.

Treatment involves a trip to the vet, who will empty the glands manually. It is important to do this without delay or they could become infected.

Dental problems

Dental problems are becoming increasingly common in dogs, and can cause serious discomfort. Good dental hygiene will do much to minimize problems with gum infection and tooth decay. If tartar accumulates to the extent that you cannot remove it by brushing, your dog will need to be anesthetized for a dental cleaning by the veterinarian.

Diarrhea

There are many reasons why a dog might have diarrhea, but most commonly it is the result of scavenging, a sudden change of diet, or an adverse reaction to a particular type of food.

If your dog is suffering from diarrhea, the first step is to withhold food for a day. It is important that he does not become dehydrated, so make sure fresh drinking water is available. However, drinking too much can increase the diarrhea, which may be accompanied with vomiting, so limit how much he drinks at any one time.

After allowing the stomach to rest, feed a bland diet, such as white fish or chicken with boiled rice for a few days. In most cases, your dog's motions will return to normal and you can resume normal feeding, although this should be done gradually.

However, if this fails to work and the diarrhea persists for more

than a few days, you should consult your vet. Your dog may have an infection, which needs to be treated with antibiotics, or the diarrhea may indicate some other problem that needs expert diagnosis.

Ear infections

The Miniature Schnauzer has neat V-shaped ears that either drop forward or are cropped to stand up. Either way, air can circulate freely, so Schnauzers are not so prone to ear infections that are more common in breeds with drop ears.

A healthy ear is clean, with no sign of redness or inflammation, and no evidence of a waxy brown discharge or a foul odor. If you see your dog scratching her ear, shaking her head, or holding one ear at an odd angle, you will need to consult your vet. The most likely causes are ear mites, an infection, or there may be a foreign body, such as a grass seed, trapped in the ear.

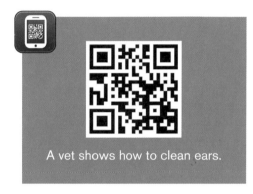
A vet shows how to clean ears.

Depending on the cause, treatment is with medicated ear drops, possibly containing antibiotics. If a foreign body is suspected, the vet will need to carry out further investigation.

Eye problems

The Miniature Schnauzer has medium eyes that are set forward. They do not protrude, and so are not especially vulnerable to injury.

If your Schnauzer's eyes look red and sore, he is likely to be suffering from conjunctivitis. This may or may not be accompanied by a watery or a crusty discharge. Conjunctivitis can be caused by a bacterial or viral infection, it could be the result of an injury, or it may be a reaction to pollen. You will need to consult your vet. Treatment with medicated eye drops is effective.

Conjunctivitis may also be the first sign of more serious inherited eye problems, which will be discussed later in this chapter.

In some instances, a dog may suffer from a dry, itchy eye, which he may further injure by scratching. This condition, known as keratoconjunctivitis sicca, may be inherited.

Foreign bodies

In the home, puppies—and some older dogs—cannot resist chewing anything that looks interesting. The toys you choose for your dog should be suitably robust to withstand damage, but children's toys can be irresistible.

Some dogs will chew—and swallow—anything from socks and other items from the laundry basket to golf balls and stones from the garden. Obviously, these items are indigestible and could cause an obstruction in your dog's intestine, which is potentially lethal.

The signs to look for are vomiting and a tucked-up posture. The dog will often be restless and will look as if he is in pain. In this situation, you must get your dog to the vet without delay, as surgery will be needed to remove the obstruction.

Heatstroke

All dogs can overheat on hot days, and this can have disastrous consequences. When the temperature rises, make sure your dog always has access to shady areas, and wait for a cooler part of the day before going for a walk. Never leave

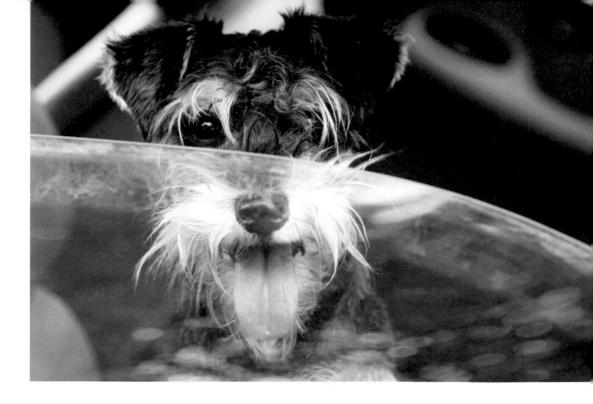

your dog in the car, as the temperature can rise dramatically—even on a cloudy day. Heatstroke can happen very rapidly, and unless you are able lower your dog's temperature, it can be fatal.

The signs of heatstroke include heavy panting and difficulty breathing, bright red tongue and mucous membranes, thick saliva, and vomiting. Eventually, the dog becomes progressively unsteady and passes out.

If your dog appears to be suffering from heatstroke, this is a true emergency. Lie him flat and then cool him as quickly as possible by hosing him down or covering him with wet towels. As soon as he has made some recovery, take him to the vet.

Lameness or limping

There are a wide variety of reasons why a dog might go lame, from a simple muscle strain to a fracture, ligament damage, or more complex problems with the joints, including inherited disorders. It takes an expert to make a correct diagnosis, so if you are concerned about your dog, do not delay in seeking help.

As your dog becomes elderly, he may suffer from arthritis, which you will see as general stiffness, particularly when he gets up after resting. It will help if you ensure his bed is in a warm, draft-free location, and if your Miniature Schnauzer gets wet after exercise, be sure to dry him thoroughly.

If your elderly dog seems to be in pain, consult your vet, who will be able to help with pain relief medication and nutritional supplements.

Skin problems

If your dog is scratching or nibbling at his skin, first check that he is free from fleas. There are other external parasites that cause itching and hair loss, but you will need a vet to help you find the culprit.

The Miniature Schnauzer is prone to allergic skin conditions. This may take the form of intense itching or hot spots. It can be quite an

undertaking to find the cause of the allergy, and you will need to follow your vet's advice, which often requires eliminating specific ingredients from the diet, as well as looking at environmental factors.

Inherited disorders

Like all purebred dogs, the Miniature Schnauzer does have a few breed-related disorders. If your dog is diagnosed with any of the diseases listed here, it is important to remember that they can affect offspring, so it is not wise to breed affected dogs.

There are now recognized screening tests that enable breeders to check for carrier and affected individuals, and hence reduce the prevalence of these diseases within the breed. DNA testing is also becoming more widely available, and as research into genetic diseases progresses, more DNA tests are being developed.

Eye disorders

In the United States, the Companion Animal Eye Registry (CAER) provides a database of dogs who have been examined by diplomates of the American College of Veterinary Ophthalmologists. The Miniature Schnauzer may be affected by the following conditions:

Progressive retinal atrophy is a bilateral degenerative disease of the cells of the retina, leading initially to night blindness and progressing to complete loss of vision. Dogs are affected from three to four years of age, and there is no treatment. There is a test available for younger dogs, before being bred, to prevent carriers from passing on the genetic defect.

Hereditary cataracts cloud the lens of your dog's eyes. They can appear in either or both eyes. Two forms of inherited cataracts have been recognized in the Miniature Schnauzer. The congenital form is inherited as a recessive trait; puppies can be assessed for it at six to eight weeks old. The developmental form of hereditary cataracts occurs in young or middle-aged dogs and can be diagnosed from six months of age. CAER recommends annual testing.

Some cataracts are small and do not grow, some grow slowly, but others can render your dog blind in a short time. Because hereditary cataracts can progress quickly, your veterinarian might recommend surgery earlier than they would on a dog with a non-genetically-based cataract. The surgery is complicated and has a relatively long recovery time, but typically an excellent outcome.

Retinal dysplasia affects the structure in the back of the eye that receives light and converts it into an electrical signal, which is then transmitted to the brain. In dogs with retinal dysplasia, the retina is malformed in some way.

In mild cases, you may not see any signs. The dog may have small blind areas, and he will be able to easily adjust. In moderate to severe cases, the dog's vision is more seriously affected, or he may be blind.

There are several forms of the disease that Miniature Schnauzers suffer from, varying in severity. Retinal dysplasia can be detected as early as six to eight weeks on examination. However, because the eye is small and young puppies are often wiggling during examination, a six-month recheck is recommended.

Hemophilia A

Hemophilia is the most common disorder of blood coagulation, inherited in a sex-linked recessive gene. This means that the male is either affected or clear, while females can be unaffected carriers for the trait. Hemophilia has been found in most dog breeds.

There are many ways in which hemophilia A can manifest, at worst as sudden death. There may be early indications, such as prolonged bleeding when the baby teeth are lost or unexpected bruising under the skin. A problem may not become apparent until after surgery, such as routine neutering or an injury. Treatment will often require a blood transfusion.

Schnauzer comedo syndrome

This is an inherited skin condition that appears to be confined to Miniature Schnauzers. It is usually spotted after clipping, and is a form of folliculitis—an infection that begins in the hair follicles. Large blackheads form, typically running down the middle of the back.

This condition is unsightly rather than serious, but it can be uncomfortable for the dog. Veterinary treatment is required in the case of bacterial infection, and may include antibiotics and medicated baths. Dogs suffering from this syndrome should not be bred.

Hyperlipidemia

This is the inability to process fats properly, causing too many lipids to circulate in the blood. Mini Schnauzers usually develop the condition by age four. The genetic basis of this disease is still not fully understood. It is usually controlled with a low-fat diet, which the dog will need to eat for life. Pancreatitis—inflammation of the pancreas that causes severe pain and gastrointestinal upset—is assumed to be associated with hyperlipidemia in the breed.

Mycobacterium avium complex

This is an extremely rare but lethal defect of the immune system that results in overwhelming systemic infection. The incidence is extremely low, but disease is lethal. There is a DNA test to screen for it.

Portosystemic shunt

These liver shunts are abnormal veins that enable blood from the intestines to bypass the liver. As a result, toxins are not removed from circulation. The treatment of choice is surgical repair, although this is not always possible. Affected dogs should not be bred.

Urolithiasis

This refers to stones in the urinary tract. The most common are struvite, occurring in the bladder. Struvite urolithiasis is very treatable with a change in diet to acidify the urine. Very large stones that obstruct the urinary tract will have to be removed surgically.

Summing up

This has been a long list of health problems, but it was not my intention to scare you. Acquiring some basic knowledge is an asset, as it will allow you to spot signs of trouble at an early stage. Early diagnosis very often leads to the most effective treatment.

The Miniature Schnauzer as a breed is a generally healthy, energetic dog with a zest for life, and annual check-ups will be all he needs. As a companion, he will bring many happy memories in the years you will spend together.

Find Out More

Books

Bradshaw, John. *Dog Sense: How the New Science of Dog Behavior Can Make You a Better Friend to Your Pet.* New York: Basic Books, 2014.

Canova, Ali, Joe Canova, and Diane Godspeed. *Agility Training for You and Your Dog: From Backyard Fun to High-Performance Training.* New York: Lyons Press, 2008.

Eldredge, Debra M., DVM, Liisa D. Carlson, DVM, Delbert G. Carlson, DVM, and James M. Giffin, MD. *Dog Owner's Home Veterinary Handbook.* 4th Ed. New York: Howell Book House, 2007.

Frier-Murza, Jo Ann. *Earthdog Ins and Outs: Guiding Natural Instincts for Success in Earthdog Tests and Den Trials,* 2nd Ed. New York: VGF Publications, 2010.

Stilwell, Victoria. *Train Your Dog Positively: Understand Your Dog and Solve Common Behavior Problems Including Separation Anxiety, Excessive Barking, Aggression, Housetraining, Leash Pulling, and More!* Berkeley: Ten Speed Press, 2013.

Websites

www.akc.org American Kennel Club

amsc.us The American Miniature Schnauzer Club

www.petmd.com PetMD

www.ukcdogs.com United Kennel Club

agility   in this case, a canine sport in which dogs navigate an obstacle course

breed standard   a detailed written description of the ideal type, size, shape, colors, movement, and temperament of a dog breed

conforms   aligns with, agrees with

docked   cut or shortened

dysplasia   a structural problem with the joints, when the bones do not fit properly together

heatstroke   a medical condition in which the body overheats to a dangerous degree

muzzle   (n) the nose and mouth of a dog; (v) to place a restraint on the mouth of a dog

neuter   to make a male dog unable to create puppies

parasites   organisms that live and feed on a host organism

pedigree   the formal record of an animal's descent, usually showing it to be purebred

socialization   the process of introducing a dog to as many different sights, sounds, animals, people and experiences as possible, so he will feel comfortable with them all

spay   to make a female dog unable to create puppies

temperament   the basic nature of an animal, especially as it affects their behavior

Index